Original title:
The Island in Your Heart

Copyright © 2025 Creative Arts Management OÜ
All rights reserved.

Author: Evan Hawthorne
ISBN HARDBACK: 978-1-80581-655-3
ISBN PAPERBACK: 978-1-80581-182-4
ISBN EBOOK: 978-1-80581-655-3

Heartstrings Tied in Nautical Knots

In your chest, a vessel swings,
With sails of laughter, joy it brings.
A compass spinning, pointing true,
Anchored safety, just me and you.

We dance on waves of playful wit,
Each wave a pun, we never quit.
Life's a tide, it ebbs and flows,
In stormy weather, humor grows.

A seagull squawks, it steals a fry,
You throw it back, we both just sigh.
The ocean's vast, but we don't fret,
With your punchlines, I'm sure to get.

So grab the line, let's ride the breeze,
Through buoyant jokes and memories.
In playful depths, our laughter swirls,
No other world, just you and pearls.

A Cove of Untold Stories

In a corner where secrets giggle,
Sandcastles rise, but they quickly wiggle.
Laughter echoes with a splash and a boom,
Tales of fish wearing hats in the room.

Mermaids in sunglasses, sipping on juice,
Dancing with dolphins, what's their excuse?
Seagulls chat gossip, oh what a show,
In this cove of wonder, where wild tales grow.

Navigating the Depths of Feeling

A ship made of giggles sails the blue,
With a crew that finds joy in every clue.
Navigating waves of laughter and cheer,
Mapping out feelings, while munching on beer.

The captain sings out, "Oh, what a sight!"
When jellyfish waltz in the pale moonlight.
Who knew emotions could float so well?
With a hearty laugh, let the stories swell.

Gentle Breezes of Forgotten Memories

Waves whisper softly, tickle the shore,
Where old socks and flip-flops call out for more.
A breeze carries scents of barbecue fun,
While crabby old crabs dance under the sun.

From swings made of coconuts, stories unfold,
Of pirates who traded their gold for some mold.
Tickled by nostalgia, so carefree and merry,
With breezes that laugh like an old sweet cherry.

Castaway in Your Embrace

A castaway dreams of a blanket so warm,
With pillows of fluff, away from the storm.
Wrapped up in giggles, I sail 'round the bend,
In a world of whimsy, with you as my friend.

Together we build dreams from clouds made of cream,
Chasing the sunlight like a wild, silly dream.
In this cozy adventure, where worries take flight,
You're the compass of joy, my heart's shining light.

The Compass of Your Emotions

When you laugh like a seal on a rock,
The directions get lost in the shock.
Your feelings, they twist like a pretzel,
As your heart plays a game, turning feral.

A map made of jelly, it wobbles a lot,
Attraction feels like a spicy hot spot.
Following whims like a puppy on a track,
Your emotions lead forward, then pull you back.

A Retreat from Reality

In a hammock that swings like a giant's grin,
You sip on daydreams brewed with a spin.
Reality's outside, trying to peek in,
But you're too busy with the giggles and din.

With coconut hats and sunscreen for flair,
You dance with the shadows, no worry or care.
The world may be wild, but here it's a treat,
Where laughter resounds and the air is sweet.

Tranquility's Embrace

In a corner of calm, where the seagulls sing,
You tuck in your heart like a curious thing.
Each wave that rolls in brings a tickling doubt,
But tranquility whispers, 'Just let it out.'

With fish in a bowl wearing hats of their own,
You join in their fun, feel the sweetness grown.
Life's like a joke in a poet's light jest,
Wrapped in warm laughter, you find your best.

Whims of the Heart's Drift

Emotions float by like balloons in the breeze,
Bursting with laughter, they dance with such ease.
The heart throws a party, confetti in tow,
As the whimsy invitingly steals the show.

In a sea made of giggles, the current's a tease,
It tickles your toes while it sways with the trees.
Though navigation's tricky, the fun's a sure thing,
You'll sail on good humor, what joy it does bring.

Coral Reefs of Warmth and Comfort

In a sea of socks and missing shoes,
A treasure map of mismatched blues.
Forget the sun, we laugh in shade,
With half-eaten snacks in our grand parade.

We're swimming in chaos, a splash and a joke,
Diving deep in a sea of smoke.
Crabs in our pockets, tales that we weave,
In this wacky dream, we never leave.

Distant Shores of Yearning

Oh to be somewhere colorful and bright,
Instead I'm here, in a sock fight.
My heart is a ship, lost in the fog,
Sailing on the waves of a retrieving dog.

I long for sunbeams, a hammock's embrace,
But here's just a cat with a goofy face.
Chasing at dreams can bring you to tears,
Especially when they involve snacks and beers.

The Stillness of Your Presence

Your laughter dances like waves on the sand,
It's sweet, it's silly, just like a band.
In stillness, we rock as the world spins around,
Like two peas in a pod, we're eternally bound.

We sit on our thrones made of pillows and fluff,
Talking of nonsense and all things tough.
The echoes of giggles fill up the room,
Transforming the silence into a bloom.

Cradle of Starlit Wishes

Under the blanket where dreams come alive,
We float like balloons, we laugh and we strive.
Stars fill our eyes as we toss and we play,
Shooting for wishes that float into sway.

The moon peeks in, with a wink and a grin,
Slumber parties start, let the games begin!
In the cradle of night, weird stories are spun,
Enchanted by laughter, two hearts become one.

A Solitary Wave in a Sea of Souls

A wave appeared, all dressed in blue,
Did a little dance, oh what a view.
It swirled and swayed, quite out of place,
Waving at fish with a silly face.

It splashed on shore, a giggling spree,
Shook off its salt and yelled, "Look at me!"
The crabs just chuckled, the seagulls flew,
While the wave kept rolling, oh, what a crew.

Footprints in the Sand of Time

Two footprints waltzed, in soft warm sand,
One looked back, had a stick in hand.
"Why did you slip?" the other did pout,
"I tripped on a crab—I thought it would shout!"

They danced along, pretending to glide,
As seagulls swooped low, they quickened their stride.
With each silly joke, they left behind,
A sandy tale that was one of a kind.

Heart-shaped Horizons

A sunset beamed, a cheeky glow,
Flirting with clouds that liked to show.
A heart-shaped horizon flicked its tail,
Turning the evening into a tale.

The colors chuckled, each shade a tease,
Tickling the stars with a gentle breeze.
"Oh look!" one laughed, as the moon took flight,
"Another giggle from our favorite night!"

The Refuge of Your Echoing Laughter

Laughter echoed in the breezy air,
Went bouncing around without a care.
It tickled the trees with a jolly sprout,
And hugged the rocks in a giggling rout.

The clouds joined in, a fluffy parade,
Raining down smiles as the jokes cascaded.
"More, more!" they cheered, as the sun peeked bright,
Casting a glow on their funny delight.

The Treasure Map of Connection

I found a map that leads to glee,
With dotted lines and an old palm tree.
X marks the spot where friendships bloom,
With laughter echoing in every room.

A compass made of silly jokes,
Navigates through giggles and pokes.
The treasure chest is full of cheer,
Buried deep with memories dear.

From pirates' tales of wild escapades,
To treasure hunts with funny parades.
Who knew connection could be so bright?
It's a hidden gem, pure delight.

So grab your hat, let's set sail,
On a quest where joy won't fail.
With every stop, a smile to share,
In this adventure beyond compare.

Waves of Untold Stories

Waves crash in with tales to tell,
Of seagulls who act like they know well.
They squawk and dive, a comedic flight,
As tides bring laughter, oh what a sight!

The ocean sings of sunburned blokes,
Wearing flip-flops and cracking jokes.
Dancing crabs on the sandy shore,
Their rhythm gets us wanting more.

Stories swirl like shells in the breeze,
Drifting close, they aim to please.
Each splash a giggle, each foam a grin,
With untold stories tucked within.

So come and join the sandy fun,
In the sun, where we all run.
With waves of laughter that never cease,
In this sea of joy, we find our peace.

Driftwood Notes

On the shore, driftwood lies piled high,
Carved with scribbles, you can't deny.
Each piece tells stories of sea and sun,
With quirky sketches, all in good fun.

A message in a bottle floats by,
Whispering secrets with a cheeky sigh.
Join me as we read what's said,
About the mermaids and their daily bread!

Sea turtles leaving silly trails,
While starfish giggle, sharing tales.
Nature's laughter fills the air,
In this wooden world, nothing compares.

So gather 'round this beachy stage,
Where every grain sparks a new page.
With driftwood notes, let our hearts soar,
In this whimsical world, who could ask for more?

Twilight's Embrace

As twilight paints the sky with glee,
Chasing stars while sipping tea.
The fireflies dance with a winking light,
Turning dusk into a playful night.

Silly shadows leap and prance,
On the grass, they start to dance.
With every flicker, giggles burst,
In this twilight, we quench our thirst.

Beneath the moon, our laughter rings,
As crickets join, playing strings.
With mischief in the starry dome,
In this embrace, we find our home.

So let's toast to the silly and absurd,
In this twilight where joy is stirred.
With each moment, our spirits lift,
In the dusk, a perfect gift.

The Sanctuary of Hidden Desires

In a cozy nook, I think of cake,
When fruitful fancies make me quake.
The secret stash, all piled so high,
Chocolate glimmers catch my eye.

With a squishy sofa, I do ignite,
Dreams of snacks that feel so right.
Whispers of chips, they tease and beg,
While I devour and take a leg.

Oh how I laugh, my belly's plight,
Saying 'Just one more' every night!
These quirky cravings, they make me cry,
As I waddle off with a satisfied sigh.

Hidden desires on a pantry shelf,
Cheeky thoughts of sneaking for myself.
In this sanctuary, I find my peace,
A world where hunger takes its lease.

Ebbing Currents of Reflection

Meet the tides that flow and sway,
Splashing water in a playful way.
Thoughts drift like boats in silly curls,
As I ponder snack time and twirling swirls.

With a rubber duck afloat my mind,
Memories of summer's fun, unwind.
Reflections dance upon the wave,
I laugh at choices I can't quite save.

Giggles echo in the gentle breeze,
Chasing sunsets that tease and squeeze.
Each wave a joke, each splash a cheer,
A tickle of laughter that we hold dear.

So hold your thoughts, let worries slide,
In these currents, we joyfully ride.
Life's a beach of jests and play,
As laughter carries worries away.

Serenity's Breath in Still Waters

Still waters brim with hope and jest,
Yet frogs still croak like they're possessed.
In this quiet, giggles bloom,
As nature whispers of a silent room.

Reflections ripple with shiny glee,
A fishy face swims up to see.
With every splash, the laughter grows,
In stillness, how the funny flows!

As clouds parade on this calm stage,
Birds chirp loudly, breaking the cage.
With a cheeky grin and a wink so bright,
Nature smirks at the fleeting light.

So take a breath, let worries drift,
In still waters, find the gift.
Life is funny, silly, and true,
In every moment, laugh anew.

Where Time Stands Still

Tick-tock, what's that silly sound?
A clock that leaps and bounds around.
In this timeless space, I find some fun,
Playing tag with shadows, everyone!

The sun may pause, as we both giggle,
With every second, there's a wiggle.
Silly dances in the vibrant light,
As moments freeze in pure delight.

Jumping rope with dreams that soar,
While clocks stop for a goofy score.
This whimsical world is bright and bold,
Where stories of laughter are retold.

Time stands still, yet giggles rise,
In dizzy spells, we claim the skies.
Embrace the fun, let worries spill,
In this laughter-filled, endless thrill.

Driftwood and Heartstrings

On a beach of flipped coins, we play,
Each wave a joke, come what may.
We laugh as the seagulls conspire,
While crabs throw shade, never tire.

Your laughter's a treasure, hard to find,
With sand stuck to cheeks, oh so blind.
We build castles with a silly face,
And drown in the giggles, a sweet embrace.

Tidal Rhythms of Affection

Waves roll in with a splashy tune,
They tickle our toes beneath the moon.
We dance with the seashells, what a sight,
Creating a ruckus, much to our delight.

Your heart beats like the ocean's roar,
While dolphins join in, who could ask for more?
Coral reefs giggle as we splish and splash,
Painting bright dreams in a bubbly bash.

Moonlight Over Calm Waters

Reflecting the mischief of goofy smiles,
We paddle our boats across the miles.
Stars throw a party, so bright and grand,
While fish whisper secrets on the soft sand.

With every ripple, a tickle and tease,
We catch the breeze, with giggles, we squeeze.
Your jokes ride the currents, swirling around,
In our shimmering realm where laughter is found.

The Lighthouse of Your Quiet Grace

A beacon that winks with a cheeky light,
Guiding our dreams through the silly night.
With a wink, it shouts, 'Don't take it too hard!'
As waves roll on, our laughter's a card.

You trip over dreams on the way to the shore,
But that's just part of the fun and the lore.
In this goofy adventure, we find our place,
With a lighthouse giggle and lots of grace.

The Song of Whales' Serenade

In the ocean's wide, blue embrace,
Whales sing tunes that make fish race.
They bubble and giggle in deep waves,
While dolphins dance like little knaves.

Seagulls join with a caw and a flap,
Mistaking a whale for an oversized nap.
Their melodies echo, a comical tune,
While squids shake their tentacles beneath the moon.

Jellyfish groove like they own the show,
Wobbling around, putting on a glow.
Octopuses crack jokes with eight-armed flair,
While shells roll their eyes, unable to care.

So in the sea's chorus, laugh we must,
For nature's jesters thrive, it's a must.
In aquatic cabarets, joy takes a part,
And every splash sings of an open heart.

A Map of Uncharted Emotions

X marks the spot where the giggles lie,
Hidden treasures where laughter can fly.
With a compass of chuckles and joy in tow,
We navigate paths where the silly winds blow.

Sudden storms of laughter, oh, what a sight,
On the shores of confusion, we dance with delight.
A lighthouse of snickers guides our way back,
Through waters of whimsy, we'll never lack.

With emotions like jellybeans, colors so bright,
We map out adventures from morning to night.
A treasure chest full of smiles awaits,
Unlocking the joy, oh, it never abates.

So gather your friends, set out for the quest,
With humor our guide, we know we're the best.
This map of our feelings leads straight to the start,
The journey's a whimsy straight from the heart.

Dewdrops of Dawn on Sandy Streets

Morning light sprinkles on sandy lanes,
Dewdrops laugh as they roll down like trains.
Footprints of crabs leave giggling trails,
As the sun rises high and the banter prevails.

Seashells gossip about secrets untold,
While ticklish grains of sand unfold.
The ocean whispers jokes in salty air,
And laughter echoes from everywhere.

Surfers tumble with grace, like clumsy pets,
Waves nudge them gently with playful bets.
Dewdrops twinkle like rude little sprites,
In a festival of humor, oh, what delights!

So let's stroll the shores with a chuckle or two,
Every wave has a punchline, waiting for you.
In this comedy act, we'll be free and neat,
With dewdrops of dawn on our sandy street.

Eclipsed Stars of Remembrance

Up above, the stars giggle shyly at night,
Veiled in a cloak, hiding from our sight.
They twinkle with secrets and comical charms,
While the moon thumbs its nose, luring us into arms.

When memories dance like fireflies in flight,
Eclipsed by laughter, they spark pure delight.
A wink from the sun, a nudge from the moon,
Together they jest, making hearts a commune.

Galaxies giggle, swirling round and round,
In cosmic comedy, joy knows no bound.
With each twinkling star, we share a good laugh,
Charting our dreams on a cosmic graph.

So raise your eyes to the skies high above,
For even within darkness, we find a sweet love.
In the echoes of cosmos, our spirits ignite,
As eclipsed stars giggle and lighten the night.

Solitary Shores of Reflection

On a beach where seagulls squawk,
I whisper to shells as they mock.
The sun shines bright with all its might,
Yet sand crabs dance out of sheer fright.

A coconut drops with a thud,
I ponder how funny life's flood.
With waves that seem to gossip and tease,
I giggle at crabs trying to freeze.

Laughter echoes from a nearby kite,
That soars and dives with pure delight.
I wave to fish that swim with glee,
Saying, 'Life's best moments are free!'

So here I sit on this sunny shore,
Telling tales of the day before.
With each splash of water, I grin,
Life's funny moments are tucked within.

Celestial Compass of the Heart

A star fell down on my funny bone,
It rolled away with a cheeky tone.
I chased it down through the night sky,
As it giggled, oh how I did try!

The moon laughed hard, oh what a sight,
As I stumbled into a tree in fright.
'Is this love or simply my luck?'
I chuckled, thinking, 'What the …' stuck!

Constellations wink with a wink,
While comets zoom past faster than I think.
I jotted notes on a napkin grand,
Scribbling jokes that I couldn't stand.

Each twinkle whispers secrets sweet,
Of dance parties held with two left feet.
Under this sky, I can't help but smile,
For laughter is the best way to travel a mile.

Hallowed Ground of Intimacy

My kitchen's a stage for culinary fun,
With a spatula mic, I'm number one.
I stir the pot with a song and a cheer,
And the dog rolls his eyes, 'Oh not this fear!'

Flour flies like confetti in the air,
But my dinner guests, well, they don't care.
They laugh at my burning casserole yells,
Between bites of chips, and unmarked gels.

It's a dance of friendship under the lights,
With roasted marshmallows and giggly bites.
We toast to the antics and funny mishaps,
While recounting past stories that fill our gaps.

So here's to the blunders that bind us tight,
With laughter that lingers, oh what a night!
In hallowed spaces where joy can thrive,
We share our hearts and the fun come alive.

Serene Waters of Remembrance

The pond reflects memories so bright,
Of skipping stones that take flight.
With each splash, a story unfolds,
Like laughter echoing from the old folds.

Frogs croak in harmony, a silly band,
As I slip on a rock, oh isn't life grand?
The ducks paddle by with a knowing glance,
I chuckle at nature, and join in the dance.

Old boats float with stories unsaid,
Of mischievous pranks, the laughter we bred.
I recall the joys wrapped in this shimmer,
As the sun fades and the lights begin to glimmer.

So here I sit, at twilight's embrace,
With memories floating, a joyful chase.
Life's silly moments, forever I'll keep,
In the serene waters that lull me to sleep.

Navigating the Current of Love

In this boat made of hopes, we sail,
Waves of your laughter bring wind to the veil.
Row past the shores where confusion resides,
But watch out for currents that tickle and slide.

The map of your smiles, so twisted and neat,
Leads to treasure chests where our shadows meet.
With paddles of whimsy, we navigate fate,
Just hold on tight, it's a hilarious fate!

Sunsets of Unfulfilled Wishes

As the sun dips low in a sky painted pink,
We scramble for wishes like kids at the brink.
Each one a giggle, a wink, and a grin,
But they fly like balloons, where do we begin?

They dance in the dusk like they're late for a show,
While we chase fleeting dreams, oh, where did they go?
With popcorn and chuckles, we savor the view,
In this comedy act painted shades of hue.

Nestled in the Echoes of You

In the blankets of your laughter, I find my retreat,
Wrapped in tickles and fun, life feels so sweet.
Echoes of joy bounce from wall to wall,
Like a mischievous sprite, they trip and they sprawl.

Your quirks are the lullabies that cradle me tight,
Singing sweet nothings into the soft night.
Nestled between memories, we create a rhyme,
Where silly meets cozy, oh, what a good time!

Coral Reefs of Warmth

Beneath the surface of giggles we dive,
To coral reefs where good vibes come alive.
With bubbles of laughter, we swim in delight,
And tickle the fish, oh, what a sight!

Warmth of your presence, a sunbeam's embrace,
In the ocean of humor, you're my favorite place.
With jests that float by like shells in the tide,
Our underwater kingdom, where joy cannot hide.

Flowing Streams of Tenderness

A river flows with silly dreams,
Fish wearing hats and bursting seams.
Turtles dance in a wacky spree,
While frogs argue over who is free.

Lemons wear glasses, chilling on a rock,
Waves bring laughter, they laugh and gawk.
With every splash, the giggles rise,
Nature plays pranks, what a surprise!

The ducks throw parties, quack like pros,
Sing karaoke in rainbow clothes.
Sandcastles crumble like a silly tease,
As seagulls laugh, they just can't cease.

Here in the waters, life's quite a joke,
Giggles erupt where laughter's bespoke.
The currents swirl with comical cheer,
Each ripple a chuckle, crystal clear!

The Colors of Distant Shores

On distant shores where hues collide,
A crab in pajamas passes with pride.
Fish wear sweaters knitted in style,
While starfish practice their ain't we wild?

Seashells gossip, in colors so bright,
Talking about clams that danced through the night.
The sunset chuckles, paints skies of corn,
Pinks and oranges, never forlorn.

Waves race the kite, 'let's see who's faster',
A dolphin jumps in, a slippery master.
Paintbrush waves on the canvas so full,
Where each splash is art, but never too dull.

All creatures here share jokes that they find,
A comedy sketch, nature so kind.
Life in the colors of amusing sights,
Bringing joy underneath the lights!

Raindrops on Calm Seas

Raindrops tumble like clumsy clowns,
Puddles reflect the smiles of towns.
Each drop a giggle, falling down fast,
Creating ripples as they amass.

Clouds are belly laughing, big and round,
While umbrellas dance as they touch the ground.
Splashes echo silly songs to repeat,
Barefoot children splatter, oh what a treat!

The ocean whispers jokes to the shore,
Waving its arms, begging for more.
Sailboats tiptoe, trying not to slip,
As rain plays tag, with a splashy trip.

Under gray skies, funny tales abound,
Every raindrop whispers joys profound.
Nature's laughter falls, pure delight,
In droplets of humor, everything's bright!

Sheltering Palm Fronds of Peace

Beneath the palms, the shadows sway,
Coconuts play hide and seek all day.
A squirrel juggles snacks, quite the feat,
While chattering birds form a comedy greet.

Cool breezes whisper funny old tales,
Of pirates and parrots with colorful sails.
Shells collect laughter, laid out in rows,
As drifters share stories like friends in prose.

The breeze tickles leaves, makes them dance,
Palm fronds join in for a merry prance.
Under the sun, they chuckle with glee,
Sharing sweet secrets, just you and me.

In nature's embrace, we all find a tune,
With humor that brightens like sun in June.
Peace dwells within, under the shade's cue,
Where laughter and joy invite all anew!

Resilient Shores of Love

On sandy banks where giggles flow,
We build our dreams with tools of glow.
Our castles made of silly schemes,
Bring laughter's tide to all our dreams.

Waves of joy crash with some grace,
Seaweed dances, join the race.
With every splash, we start to grin,
In this wild frolic, we begin.

Funny seashells in a line,
Whisper secrets of the divine.
We'll sail our boat made of delight,
Tugging hearts with all our might.

Under starry skies, we toast,
To silly moments we adore most.
The tide of laughter will not fade,
In our little world, we've made.

Breath of Breeze in Stillness

A gentle puff on a lazy day,
Swirling chuckles come out to play.
With whispers soft as cotton candy,
Breezes tickle; oh, how dandy!

Invisible hands guide us around,
Chasing giggles that swirl profound.
The wind's a tricky little trickster,
Bringing smiles like a jolly twister.

Clouds of fluff that float so high,
Make room for joy, oh me, oh my!
When the stillness holds its breath,
We share our laughs till nothing's left.

Whirling thoughts like autumn leaves,
Sprinkling joy through all it weaves.
In every gust, we find a song,
In this breeze, we all belong.

Notes of Laughter in the Breeze

A jolly tune in the air does play,
With giggles fluttering far away.
Little birds join, they sing along,
To the rhythm of our joyful song.

Twirly dances, butterflies prance,
Nature winks, it's a funny chance.
Each note springs forth like bouncy flares,
Filling hearts with silly cares.

As kite tails twirl with fidgety flair,
Joyful echoes hang in the air.
Laughter weaves through grassy fields,
A delight that the daylight yields.

With every chuckle, the sun will shine,
In the breeze, our spirits align.
Notes of laughter, a sweet refrain,
In this dance, there's nothing to gain.

Boundless Waters of Connection

In endless waves of silly jest,
We paddle boats, put friendship to test.
Splashing joy, we feel so free,
In the sea of our revelry.

Floating by on inflatable dreams,
Where nothing's as silly as it seems.
We toss our fears to the playful tide,
In the laughter, we do abide.

Shining glimmers on every crest,
Remind us humor is the best.
As we drift on this glowing sea,
Boundless laughter, just you and me.

With sun-kissed smiles and waves so wide,
Together we joyfully glide.
In this sea where hearts align,
Every chuckle feels divine.

Elysian Retreat

In a realm where laughter blooms,
I found a chair made of spoons.
With jellybeans flying past,
We danced like fish, oh what a blast!

The river flows with soda pop,
Balloons above begin to plop.
Cotton candy clouds in the sky,
Oh dear, was that a flying pie?

A tree that sings when you sit down,
It croaked a joke and made us frown.
But laughter bubbled like a brook,
In this quirky, silly nook!

As sunsets spill like melted cheese,
We laughed and rolled without a tease.
This crazy place where giggles thrive,
Oh, how I wish we could forever jive!

Untamed Shores of Affection

On shores where seashells serenade,
Dance crabs in a wild charade.
With seagulls winking as they fly,
Who knew love would make us sigh?

A hammock hung from jellyfish,
I made a very goofy wish.
The waves chuckled as they crashed,
A sea of giggles, oh, how it splashed!

A pie of sand that looked quite fine,
We took a slice and called it mine.
With bubbles bouncing in the air,
Our goofy lives without a care!

And when the sunsets paint the tide,
We surfed on laughter, side by side.
With every wave that kissed the shore,
We love this madness, always more!

Caverns of Longing

In caverns deep where echoes play,
A bat once told a joke today.
With stalactites draped like hats,
We giggled at the chubby cats!

A treasure map, oh what a find,
Leads to a chest where sweets entwined.
With gummy bears and chocolate gold,
Who knew that cravings could be bold?

With shadows dancing on the walls,
The ghost of humor surely calls.
Whispers tickle every stone,
We laughed until we felt at home!

This cavern sparkles with delight,
Where even sadness takes its flight.
Our hearts a-joke, our spirits light,
In this strange cave of pure delight!

Moonlit Reflections

Under the moon's bright, silly gaze,
We danced in glittery, giggly ways.
A turtle wore a shiny hat,
And told us tales of this and that!

The lake laughed back with rippling cheer,
As frogs crooned songs that we could hear.
With fireflies teasing in a waltz,
We spun around and laughed without faults!

The stars above played peek-a-boo,
While we went searching for a shoe.
Oh, how we tumbled in delight,
On this bright and whimsical night!

With wishes whispered on the breeze,
We heard the moon crack jokes with ease.
In this wondrous, funny dream,
Life's a comedy, or so it seems!

A Haven Beyond the Waves

In a place where surfboards dance,
Seagulls plot their lunch romance.
Sandy toes and ice cream spills,
Sunburnt noses and silly thrills.

Coconuts wear silly hats,
While crabs engage in table chats.
Beach towels fly like sails so bright,
Chasing seagulls in pure delight.

Waves whisper secrets from afar,
While jellyfish swim in a bizarre.
Laughter echoes, joy unfurls,
As we splash through our own swirls.

Under stars, the night-time hums,
While we joke, the laughter comes.
With squirt guns and beach ball wars,
This paradise opens unseen doors.

Secrets Beneath the Palm Trees

Beneath the palms where secrets lie,
Squirrels play their cheeky spy.
With coconuts as their treasure trove,
And sandcastles where dreams move.

A crab in sunglasses struts with style,
While tourists stop to stare a while.
Even turtles have gossip games,
Swapping tales with silly names.

Salty air fills our every laugh,
As we play pretend with a gaff.
Mermaids giggle, a fish in disguise,
Their laughter twinkles like starry skies.

As night falls, the stars align,
Sharing snacks and summer wine.
A dance of joy, we sway and cheer,
For the secrets we hold dear.

Lost in a Sea of Dreams

Swallowed whole by daydreams, caught,
In giant waves of laughter sought.
Floating far on a floppiest board,
Hoping my sunburn won't be ignored.

Fish wear sunglasses, giving us grins,
While dolphins play with their goofy fins.
We lose track of the time and tide,
Riding the waves, we go along for the ride.

Mermaids giggle, their hair in tangles,
While I trip on shells, oh how it dangles!
A sandcastle falls, but we just scream,
For the fun brings us back to a gleam.

Under the moon, adventures restart,
With ice cream dreams filling each heart.
Lost in laughter, no worries or schemes,
Just a silly day in our wild dreams.

Echoes of Love in the Tides

Waves crash with whispers from the deep,
As crabs in couples take their leap.
Seaweed hairdos bob and sway,
As we laugh and play the day away.

Messages in bottles drift ashore,
With silly love notes we adore.
Seashells giggle, as we propose,
To ocean waves, that's how it goes!

Our shadows dance on the sandy floor,
As the sun bows out, we ask for more.
With ice cream drips and sticky hands,
We weave love stories in golden sands.

Echoes of joy, like tides, repeat,
With every laugh, our hearts compete.
As night descends, we share our dreams,
Under twilight's glow where nothing seems.

Reflections on Sunlit Waters

I set sail on a rubber duck,
With snacks piled high, oh what luck!
Sunshine paints the waves like gold,
My sailboat dreams—never too bold.

I spotted a seagull, bold and brash,
Stealing my sandwich in a flash.
I yelled, 'Hey, buddy, that's my lunch!'
He winked at me, then made a munch.

The waves giggle as they dance around,
While fish in tuxedos leap and bound.
I spot a crab with a silly hat,
Doing the cha-cha, fancy that!

With each splash, laughter fills the air,
In a world where worries just don't dare.
From sunlit waters, joy does flow,
Who knew my heart could steal the show?

The Map to Inner Serenity

I drew a map with crayons bright,
To inner peace by candlelight.
Each twist and turn, a pie-shaped slice,
With landmarks marked, oh how nice!

First stop: laughter at the creek,
Where frogs wear ties and a cute streak.
Next, a hill where tickles reign,
And giggles fall like gentle rain.

I tripped on clouds, oh what a sight,
Chasing butterflies, oh what delight!
A compass spun, I lost my way,
But found a joke—a punny ray.

With every turn, my heart does soar,
From silly hops to friendship's core.
I'll follow this map, come what may,
For laughter leads me, come play!

Adrift in a Sea of Longing

I'm drifting here on a ketchup boat,
With dreams of fries, oh what a note!
A mermaid waves, she's tasting bliss,
But all I want is a tasty dish.

The ocean's got a spicy vibe,
With pickles dancing, oh what tribe!
I dream of taco clouds up high,
And sprinkle donuts raining from the sky.

Loneliness sinks like a soggy bun,
But jellyfish sing and have some fun.
I'll trade my woes for a jester's hat,
Join a sea party, how about that?

Adrift in giggles, I find my way,
With toppings of laughter leading the play.
In this sea, I'll surf on dreams,
With silly thoughts and happy themes!

Harbor of Unraveled Dreams

In a harbor where wild dreams float,
I found a frog on a wobbly boat.
He took my hat, then struck a pose,
Said, 'Fashion's all about the toes!'

Drifting past, a cat in shades,
Sipping tea and playing charades.
His whiskers dance, his laughter rolls,
In this harbor, we find our souls.

The piers are lined with ice cream carts,
Where jokes are sold and laughter starts.
I ordered joy, a massive scoop,
They serve it fresh, a happy troupe.

From this harbor, dreams freely roam,
With jesters and joy, I've found my home.
I'll sail these waves until I gleam,
In the harbor where we chase the dream!

A Retreat to the Infinite Blue

In a sea of socks and mismatched shoes,
I found my island, sipping on a fuse.
Seagulls squawked jokes, the tide was a tease,
Laughing with the waves, life was a breeze.

Sunburned dreams and a face full of sand,
Dancing crabs applauding, oh, it's so grand.
With flip-flops flapping, I try to keep pace,
Chasing sunsets, wearing a goofy face.

A beach ball bounces, full of silly cheer,
I talk to the tide like it's a well-known peer.
Seashells whisper secrets of laughter untold,
In this paradise, I feel young and bold.

Beneath palm trees swaying, I take a big nap,
Awake to a picnic, what a splendid trap.
The folk laugh so loudly, they snort and they wheeze,
Welcome to my retreat, where everyone's at ease.

Mornings Wrapped in Warmth

A mug of cocoa, tangled hair in sight,
I trip on the rug, what a morning delight!
The cat drinks my coffee, the dog steals my toast,
In this silly chaos, I find the most.

Sunshine beams in, a watchful old friend,
Whispering good mornings, on that I depend.
The cereal's dancing, it leaps from the bowl,
A breakfast ballet, my heart's in control.

I put on mismatched socks, that's how I roll,
A wobbly dance starts, it's good for the soul.
As toast pops like fireworks, I let out a laugh,
Each morning a party, my joyful memoirs' half.

With giggles and grins, we start every day,
In the warmth of the madness, we laugh and we play.
Wrapped in happy moments, a light that won't part,
Each morning's adventure, a feast for the heart.

The Oasis of Unspoken Words

In a garden of whispers, secrets are brewed,
With plants in my hair, I'm the sun's favorite dude.
The daisies gossip, the trees have a chat,
In this wild wonder, I just tip my hat.

A cactus, a sage, give the best advice,
"Don't drown in your thoughts, just roll some dice!"
The butterflies chuckle, fluttering by,
"Why so serious? Just let out a sigh!"

With sunlight for ink, I write down my dreams,
A canvas of laughter flows in sparkling streams.
This oasis is thriving with giggles and grins,
Where the heart shares its stories, and joy always wins.

A sip of good humor fills up the air,
Join the parade, dance without a care.
In this magical realm, we speak soft and loud,
Under the stars, we sit joyfully proud.

Treasures Buried in the Heart's Breeze

A treasure map scribbled on a napkin's delight,
Find the golden giggles, not far from your sight.
With a shovel of smiles, I dig in the sand,
Who knew that my heart was a circus so grand?

The crabs join the search, wearing tiny red hats,
Murmuring riddles, avoiding the chats.
Old bottles float by with messages vague,
"What's life without laughter? Just a soggy old plague!"

Oh, treasure awaits in each goofy old tale,
The wind blows its secrets, a sailboat's prevail.
In laughter we find what our hearts long to keep,
For the greatest adventure is found in a leap.

So let's dance through the currents, let worries drift by,
Embracing the silly beneath the bright sky.
With warmth in our pockets and joy in our eyes,
We uncover the treasures where true laughter lies.

Amidst Coral Walls of Solace

In a shell that squeaks like a frightened mouse,
I found a treasure far from the grouse.
With crabs in tuxedos, they waltz on the sand,
Uninvited guests with a dance that is grand.

Seashells whisper jokes in a conch's warm hug,
I chuckle so hard that I throw out a slug.
The octopus tells me to lighten my wear,
As he juggles my worries without a care.

A fish in a bow tie serves dinner with flair,
While shrimps clank their glasses and raise them in air.
I ponder the meaning of life at the reef,
Does seaweed tickle? That's my belief!

So dance with the sea, let your laughter take flight,
Amidst these coral walls, everything feels right.
Forget all your troubles, let the waves do their part,
For joy bubbles up in this whimsical heart.

The Hidden Cove of Belonging

Nestled 'neath leaves where the coconut sways,
I met a parrot with health tips and phase.
He squawked, 'Eat more nuts, let your laughter resound!'
While squirrels played poker on soft, grassy ground.

Lizards in sunglasses just strut down the path,
Making wisecracks that lighten my wrath.
The tidepool holds secrets from all walks of life,
Like snails with their gossip and clams in mid-strife.

A crab runs a café; his coffee's a blast,
With bubbles of fun that are sure to last.
In this sunny cove, I've found my true team,
Letting giggles and smiles fulfill every dream.

So gather your pals, let the laughter commence,
In this hidden refuge, life makes perfect sense.
With every new wave, our memories grow,
Join in on the fun, let the good times flow!

Sunsets of Fading Shadows

As the sun drops low, it paints the sky red,
Soft giggles emerge from the clouds overhead.
I danced with a shadow, who tripped over time,
And laughed as it grumbled, 'Why must I rhyme?'

The crabs held a concert, their claws in the air,
With a rock band of clams, who could not find a chair.
Fireflies flicker, shining laughter and cheer,
In this fading light, worries disappear.

Whales serenade us with melodies sweet,
While gulls join in, with an off-key repeat.
A sunset's embrace feels like warm, fuzzy socks,
In this festival of colors, I dance like a fox.

So let shadows linger and twirl all around,
In this twilight laughter, happiness found.
With each fading gleam, let your spirit take flight,
For joy's in the sunset, igniting the night.

A Voyage Through Inner Waters

In a boat made of giggles, I sail through the mind,
With fishes of thoughts swirling, oh so unlined.
The waves of my worries are tickling my feet,
As dolphins perform dance moves, truly a treat.

An otter sells snacks while I paddle away,
Sipping juice from a coconut, brightening my day.
With each gentle splash, I can feel all's alright,
As the stars start to twinkle and kiss me goodnight.

I've pirated my fears, let 'em walk the plank,
Instead, I'll hoist laughter and sail with a crank.
With sea turtles sharing their wisdom and lore,
Their philosophy's simple: love life, and explore.

So aboard this fine vessel, let giggles unfurl,
In these inner waters, it's a wondrous swirl.
With each gentle ripple, let joy set the course,
In this voyage of laughter, I find my true source.

The Harbor of Dreams Yet to Come

In a boat that's quite absurd,
With oars made out of cheese,
We set sail on a whimsy word,
Chasing seagulls with the breeze.

The captain wears a pirate hat,
His map's all drawn in crayon,
He steers the ship toward a giant cat,
Who claims to be an ancient crayon.

We fish for dreams in bubblegum,
And trade them with the fish so keen,
For in this harbor, we won't succumb,
To boredom, we are the scene.

With laughter echoing far and wide,
We plunder joy and find a pearl,
In this harbor, we'll reside,
And let our merry madness swirl.

Whispers of Solitude

In a hammock tied to nothing,
I contemplate my fate,
The whispers of my sneaky cat,
Say solitude just can't wait.

She lounges like a noble queen,
My thoughts all play as jesters,
We plot a tea party scene,
With biscuits served by testers.

A rubber duck floats by the tree,
It quacks a tune so loud,
It sprinkles nonsense joyfully,
Becoming my silly crowd.

For in this quiet, laughter peeks,
Dancing through the garden's air,
In solitude, a joy that speaks,
Where fun and whimsy share a chair.

Sheltered Shores of Emotion

Upon the sand of silly times,
We sculpt mishaps in the grain,
A castle built of rhyme and chimes,
And a moat that won't contain.

The seagulls snatch our tasty fries,
And laugh as they take flight,
While crabs in tuxedos criticize,
Our picnic art, a hilarious sight.

But shark, with sunglasses on,
Winks from beneath the sea,
With sunblock and a broken lawn,
He joins our wacky spree.

So let the waves roll and dance away,
In these shores where feelings play,
We toast to laughter, bright and gay,
Sheltering dreams here every day.

Heartbeats on Tranquil Sands

With tiny footprints made of jelly,
We race the tide's return,
The ocean's rhythm makes me silly,
As my heart begins to churn.

A beach ball flies—a wild ride,
And lands upon my head,
With laughter over-saturated,
We bury worries instead.

The shells are sparkly, tales are tall,
Each one speaks in crazy tones,
A conch shell's gossip enthralls us all,
As we build castles with our phones.

So let the waves serenade,
With every giggle in the air,
On tranquil sands, memories made,
Together in joy, beyond compare.

The Paradise of Your Yearning

In a spot where piña coladas flow,
I tried to catch a sunbeam on my toe.
Yet the sand laughed as it slipped away,
And now my foot's on vacation, I must say.

A coconut dreams of being a hat,
While seagulls squawk, 'We're having a spat!'
Palm trees dance like they're in a ball,
And I'm here hoping for a beachside call.

Flip-flops whisper secrets they won't share,
While starfish plot under water, unaware.
I asked a crab for some sage advice,
He told me; 'Live life, but don't misuse my spice!'

In this place where humor takes the helm,
I found joy in forgetting where I dwell!
So let's toast to laughter, tropical and bright,
For in my heart, every day is a flight!

Sanctuary of Lost Echoes

There's a cave where echoes giggle away,
And shadows play tag till the end of the day.
I stumbled on treasures not worth a dime,
But they sure make for great stories with rhyme!

Ghost crabs lounge while sipping on tea,
Debating the merits of living carefree.
One said, 'Life's better with a wink and a jest,'
While the other just brought up a ridiculous quest.

I tried to catch whispers of yesterday's fables,
But they slipped right through like a heap of old labels.
With a sigh, I plopped down on wet mossy ground,
And resolved to embrace the laughter I found.

Here in this nook, where odd things collide,
Every lost echo is my playful guide.
In a sanctuary where witticisms reign,
Who needs solemn vows or any real gain?

Beneath the Palm of Memories

Underneath a palm that thinks it's a king,
I tried to explain my eccentric fling.
It just rustled, as if rolling its eyes,
While a parrot squawked, 'You're quite the surprise!'

I once lost my thoughts in a hammock's embrace,
Where ideas floated and danced, just like lace.
But a breeze snatched them, as cheeky as can be,
And now I'm stuck with a crab's poetry!

I thought of the times that turned into laughs,
Like juggling coconuts, all broken halves.
Though I stumbled, I twirled, I fell in the sand,
Beneath this palm, it all feels quite grand.

So here's to the moments that tickle your soul,
In a land where the silly moments are whole.
Let the currents of mischief lift your spirit high,
Underneath this palm, let's laugh till we cry!

Breeze of Unspoken Words

The breeze swirls giggles through the tall grass,
Tickling my nose, as I sit on my sass.
It whispers secrets from a world so absurd,
And I'm stuck laughing at each silly word.

Dandelions float with a fluttering cheer,
As I try to calculate how much I can hear.
They wink at the daisies, who roll their green eyes,
While the crickets play tunes that no one belies.

I nearly confessed to a wave passing by,
But it splashed me instead, oh my oh my!
Yet the laughter erupted, a soft serenade,
From the cacophony of my mishaps, I'm made.

So let the wind carry my rambling tones,
For it wraps me snug in nature's own bones.
With the breeze as my partner in whimsical play,
I'll dance through the moments, come what may!

Tides of Emotion

Waves crash in a playful dance,
Joyful splashes, we take a chance.
The seagulls cackle, oh what a sight,
Surfboards wobble, hearts take flight.

Sandcastles crumble, laughter abounds,
Shells and treasures, where fun resounds.
With each tide, a giggle erupts,
In this silly world, we're all corrupt.

Pirates in flip-flops, sailing wide,
We dodge the splashes, with arms open wide.
As sunburns bloom like confetti in air,
We roast marshmallows, without a care.

Lifesavers bobbing, a floaty parade,
Chasing our dreams in jelly-sand glade.
Mermaids giggle, under the sun,
Splashing around, oh, what fun!

Anchor of Secrets

Beneath the waves, where whispers dwell,
An anchor of secrets, oh what a sell!
Buried treasure, or just a sock?
The ocean's giggles, a playful mock.

Fish swap jokes, on a coral reef,
Clams tell tales, beyond belief.
The octopus dons a humorous hat,
While crabs do the cha-cha, imagine that!

Shells gossip loudly, as tides do shift,
With every wave, comes a new gift.
The seaweed dances, twirls in delight,
As we chase dreams, shining so bright.

Sailboats don't sail, they watch and cheer,
While dolphins perform, making it clear.
Under the moon, with laughter we bask,
The ocean's secrets, no need to ask.

Whispering Waves of Desire

Waves whisper secrets, with playful delight,
As sun-kissed bodies dance through the night.
The breeze brings giggles, a flirtatious tease,
A world of tomfoolery, at ease with the seas.

Seashells conspire, to tickle our toes,
As squids spin tales, in comical prose.
The tide brings chuckles, like bubbles in foam,
In this whirlpool of joy, we find a home.

Footprints in the sand, a dance of our fate,
The jellyfish jive, oh isn't it great?
With every splash, desires take flight,
As we laugh at the stars, in the moon's golden light.

So let's float in laughter, with glee,
In this ocean of whims, just you and me.
As whispers of waves keep our spirits high,
We'll ride this current until we touch the sky.

Beyond the Horizon of Hope

Beyond the horizon, where dreams bloom bright,
Laughter echoes, a buoyant flight.
The seagulls dive, in comical loops,
As we all join in, with silly whoops.

Rafts filled with snacks, the party's begun,
With every splash, we're almost done.
But wait! A wave gives one safe shove,
Over the edge, we tumble and shove.

Kites fly high, like wishes set free,
As we learn to dance with the ocean's decree.
Giggling merfolk sneak peeks from below,
As we wobble and whirl, putting on a show.

So here's to the journey, wherever we roam,
With laughter and joy, we'll always find home.
Beyond the horizon lies a tale still unfurled,
With every wave, a new wonder is twirled.

Paradise Found Within

In a land of socks and lost remote,
A treasure map drawn on a cereal boat.
Where jellybeans grow on candy trees,
And laughter drifts in the summer breeze.

With couches of clouds and pillows of cream,
We lounge with a joy that feels like a dream.
Penguins dance with a tap and a spin,
While the fridge is stocked with just cake and gin.

Sunshine pours like syrup on toast,
A playful dragon lets out a boast.
Every corner brings smiles so wide,
In this joyful place, who needs a guide?

So pack up your giggles, let's sail away,
To this quirky land where we laugh and play.
With every silly thought and silly glee,
In a paradise made for you and me.

The Currents of Your Gentle Touch

A tickle here, a poke right there,
The currents whirl, a whimsical affair.
With every nudge, the giggles rise,
Your gentle touch, an endless surprise.

Like jellyfish dancing in the moonlit sea,
Your fingertips spark joy, oh can't you see?
Every playful jab, a wave of delight,
In a playful world, everything feels right.

Swirls of laughter turning in space,
With each little poke, I find my place.
You're the whirlpool, I'm the boat,
Together we drift, and that's no joke.

Even the seagulls stop to laugh,
At the chaos we craft on our happy path.
A universe built on silly schemes,
Riding the currents of our wild dreams.

Sheltered from the Storms Within

In the cocoon of muffled chats,
Where thoughts bounce like curious cats.
A fortress made with pillows and fun,
Hiding from sighs, we're never done.

Sipping lemonade, we laugh at the rain,
Around us, a whirl of joy, not pain.
Storm clouds gather but can't get through,
We've built our barricade, just us two.

With half-eaten snacks and jokes so absurd,
We welcome the chaos with a silly word.
Each thunderclap a tickle and tease,
In our fortress of fun, we do as we please.

So when life's storms try to come in,
We'll giggle together, never give in.
For wrapped in laughter, we claim our crown,
In this silly kingdom, we'll never frown.

Island Dreams of the Heart

In the land of socks and mismatched shoes,
Where dreams sprout wings and chase away blues.
A hammock swings with whispers of cheer,
As our giggles float gently in the air.

We plant our wishes in a garden of jest,
With sunflowers towering, growing the best.
Ticklish vines wrap around our feet,
In our whimsical world, every day is sweet.

While squirrels perform in a comedy club,
And bananas wear hats, all part of the scrub.
Lemonade rivers flow with zest,
In this strange realm, we're simply blessed.

So let's build castles with giggles and glee,
Where mirth is the currency and fun is the key.
With hearts like balloons, we'll float and soar,
In these joyful dreams, who could ask for more?

Shores of Silent Longing

I spied a crab wearing my old hat,
He waved hello, then sat just like that.
Seashells gossip, they're quite the chatter,
I laugh at their tales, they really don't matter.

A dolphin danced, he wanted a show,
But tripped on a wave and fell below.
Seagulls squawked, declaring a feast,
I offered them fries—they called me a beast!

Tide pools sparkled, tiny fish had a ball,
I joined their parade, feeling so small.
With seaweed wigs and a splashy retreat,
We danced on the shores, it was quite the feat!

When the sun went to sleep, I bid adieu,
To my finned friends and the crab in blue.
Laughing aloud as I crept on the sand,
Who knew silent longing could feel so grand!

Castaway Dreams

I built a fine castle from driftwood and shells,
A kingdom of crabs with glimmering spells.
The tide came in, but I stood my ground,
As my sandy creation got turned upside down.

A parrot flew by, squawking with glee,
His talents outshone even the best of me.
He wore shiny beads and a crown made of leaves,
I thought, what a guy—he's got all the thie—

On coconut chairs we threw a big bash,
All the fish joined in, with some glorious splash.
A sea cucumber tried his best to impress,
But I told him, "Buddy, you just need a dress!"

The night brought a glow of the moon's funny face,
We toasted our victory—oh, what a place!
In dreams, we still revel, not a care in the sea,
For every silly castaway feels cozy and free!

Within the Cove of Solitude

I found a secluded cove all my own,
Where pebbles whispered, and sea foam was sown.
An octopus waved, trying to get my name,
But forgot it instantly—oh, what a shame!

A lawn chair appeared, just sitting there still,
I sat down right next to a crab on a hill.
We exchanged our stories—mine sparkled like dusk,
His were mostly tales of old shoelace and rust.

The day dripped away like syrup on toast,
And fish practiced ballet, oh how they would boast!
A walrus, quite jolly, joined in with a cheer,
Said, "Life's better shared, with some laughter, my dear!"

Nightfall embraced us with stars all around,
I grinned at my friends, oh, what a compound!
Laughter and joy, in our little retreat,
In solitude's embrace, we found something sweet!

Heart's Hidden Oasis

In a fountain of joy where the coconuts fall,
I spilled my secrets to a friendly sea squall.
It chuckled and burbled, made bubbles with glee,
Told me, "Don't worry, just come dance with me!"

My flip-flops went swimming, they're rebels, you see,
Joined in with the tide, not consulting with me.
A pelican's cackle echoed through the shore,
"Life's all about toes and a little bit more!"

Crabs in tuxedos were ready to dine,
With plates full of seaweed and shells that did shine.
I joined in the laughter, we dined under stars,
I'll never forget my seafood bazaar!

Though water may splash and the sea may roar,
Love's hidden oasis, a charming uproar.
From the salty embraces, I know I will part,
But I'll carry the joy in the depths of my heart!

www.ingramcontent.com/pod-product-compliance
Lightning Source LLC
Chambersburg PA
CBHW072223070526
44585CB00015B/1470